HAIKU

Classic Japanese Short Poems

amber
BOOKS

This edition first published in 2024

First published in 2016 by
Amber Books Ltd
United House
North Road
London N7 9DP
United Kingdom
www.amberbooks.co.uk
Facebook: amberbooks
YouTube: amberbooksltd
Instagram: amberbooksltd
X(Twitter): @amberbooks

ISBN: 978-1-83886-482-8

Printed and bound in China

Introduction written and poems translated by Hart Larrabee
Project Editor: Sarah Uttridge
Design: Rick Fawcett

Hart Larrabee is an American translator who lives with his family in the little
town of Obuse in northern Nagano, Japan, right in the heart of Issa country.
His translations of short stories by Fumio Takano and Mitsuyo Kakuta have
appeared, respectively, in the anthologies *Tomo: Friendship Through Fiction*
and *The Book of Tokyo: A City in Short Fiction*. He also translates non-fiction,
particularly in the fields of art, design, and architecture.

TRADITIONAL CHINESE BOOKBINDING

This book has been produced using traditional Chinese bookbinding
techniques, using a method that was developed during the Ming Dynasty
(1368–1644) and remained in use until the adoption of Western binding
techniques in the early 1900s. In traditional Chinese binding, single sheets of
paper are printed on one side only, and each sheet is folded in half, with the
printed pages on the outside. The book block is then sandwiched between
two boards and sewn together through punched holes close to the cut edges
of the folded sheets.

Crows, from *Kite and Crows*, by Yosa Buson (Kitamura Museum, Tokyo)

Formal Aspects

A Japanese poetry genre with ancient roots, haiku is more than just seventeen syllables arranged 5-7-5. Indeed, even this familiar prescription is thorny: the word 'haiku', for example, is three syllables in Japanese (ha-i-ku) but two in English (hai-ku). Translating into seventeen English syllables usually invites excessive wordiness and is not attempted here.

Japanese haiku are generally written on a single vertical line, their rhythm sufficient to reveal the shape of the poem. The translations here use three lines to reflect the pacing of the original. Haiku often include a fragment and a phrase, the former indicated by a 'cutting word' (*kireji*) – a kind of voiced punctuation – such as *ya* at the end of the first line or *kana* at the end of the third. In translation, *kireji* may be represented by a dash, an exclamation point, or left unmarked.

Haiku typically describe a moment in the present and include a 'season word' (*kigo*) that anchors the poem in time while imbuing it with both transience and timelessness. Poet and reader are united by their shared experience of nature and the changing seasons, of ageing and the passage of time.

Historical Background

Many poems we now call haiku should properly be called *hokku*: 'starting verse' that begin sequences of linked verse. *Renga* evolved during Japan's medieval period (1185–1600), extending the two-stanza (5-7-5, 7-7) form of earlier court poetry through collaborative poetic dialogue, with participants adding stanzas of alternate length up to a predetermined number. *Renga* was bound by complex rules and demanded fluency in the classics. However, a playful parallel form – *haikai no renga* (unorthodox *renga*), or just *haikai* – allowed thematic flexibility and vernacular language.

The peace and stability of the seventeenth century enabled some *renga* and *haikai* poets to make a living as teachers. More than 'high-culture' *renga*, 'low-culture' *haikai* found favour among prosperous farmers and city-dwellers, quickly developing competing schools and styles. *Hokku*, with its privileged position within the genre, came to be composed and published independently.

Matsuo Bashō (1644–1694) elevated *haikai* to the level of literature. Born to a samurai family near Kyoto, by the age of thirty he was established in Edo literary circles. Ambivalent about his success as a poet and teacher, he began studying Zen. For the last decade of his life he alternated time in Edo with journeys that produced his renowned prose-and-poetry travel diaries. His mature *hokku* style espoused 'lightness' (*karumi*), conveying spiritual depth through ordinary situations and plain language.

After Bashō's death the popularity of cruder forms of *haikai* overtook the aspirations of his followers, and in the mid-eighteenth century there was a call to return to the ideals of Bashō. Prominent among Bashō Revival poets, **Yosa Buson** (1716–1784) was born outside Osaka, moved to Edo in his twenties, then spent a decade travelling in emulation of Bashō before settling in cosmopolitan Kyoto. Better known as a painter in his time, Buson's poems present idealized images combining literary allusion with an appeal to the senses.

Kobayashi Issa (1763–1828) was born to farmers in what is now northern Nagano. His mother died when he was a child and he was sent to Edo as a teen, later travelling as an itinerant poet and becoming a lay Buddhist priest. After resolving a long-running feud with the stepmother who sought to deny him his inheritance, he returned to his childhood home late in life only to endure the death of four children and his first wife. Despite or because of such hardships, his poems are personal, playful and earthy, expressing empathy for the weak – insects, animals and children – without sentimentality.

Born in Matsuyama, **Masaoka Shiki** (1867–1902) moved to Tokyo as a student at a time of radical change as Japan opened to the west. Though bedridden with tuberculosis for years at the end, Shiki was influential as a poet and critic, decrying the indiscriminate adulation of Bashō and extolling the clarity and objectivity of Buson. Seeking to liberate Japanese poetry from the past, he established the term 'haiku' to replace *hokku*, declaring the form independent of linked verse and removing it from the realm of discourse to that of art in the modern mould.

ki o kirite
motokuchi miru ya
kyō no tsuki

The cut end of
A fresh-felled tree—
Tonight's moon

木を切りて本口見るや今日の月

夜秘かに虫は月下の栗を穿つ

yoru hisoka ni
mushi wa gekka no
kuri o ugatsu

After darkness falls
A stealthy worm burrows
Into a moonlit chestnut

かれえだ　からす
枯枝に烏のとまりけり秋の暮
あき　くれ

kare eda ni
karasu no tomarikeri
aki no kure

A crow at rest
On a leafless bough—
Autumn's twilight

五月雨に鶴の足短くなれり

samidare ni
tsuru no ashi
mijikaku nareri

The crane's legs
Grow shorter in the
Early summer rain

雲しぐれ富士をみぬ日ぞ面白き

kirishigure
fuji o minu hi zo
omoshiroki

Mist and drizzle
Fuji hidden all day—
How delightful!

蘭の香や蝶の翅に薫物す

らん か ちょう つばさ たきもの

ran no ka ya
chō no tsubasa ni
takimono su

Fragrant orchid—
Perfuming the wings
Of a butterfly

樫の木の花にかまはぬ姿かな

kashi no ki no
hana ni kamawanu
sugata kana

The oak tree
Stands unswayed
By blossoms

古池や蛙飛び込む水の音

ふるいけ　かわず　と　　こ　　みず　　おと

furuike ya
kawazu tobikomu
mizu no oto

An old pond—
The splash of
Plunging frogs

瓶割るる夜の氷の寝覚め哉

kame waruru
yoru no kōri no
nezame kana

Water jar cracks
An icy night's
Awakening

冬の日や馬上に凍る影法師

ふゆ
ひ
ばじょう
こお
かげぼうし

fuyu no hi ya
bajō ni kōru
kagebōshi

Winter sun—
Astride my horse
A frozen shadow

この螢田毎の月にくらべみん

ほたる たごと　つき

kono hotaru
tagoto no tsuki ni
kurabemin

These fireflies
So like the moons
In terraced paddies

閑さや岩にしみ入る蝉の声

shizukasa ya
iwa ni shimiiru
semi no koe

Such stillness—
The song of cicadas
Seeping into stone

初時雨猿も小蓑を欲しげなり

はつしぐれ さる こみの ほ

hatsu shigure
saru mo komino
hoshige nari

In this bleak rain
Even the monkeys seem to want
Little straw cloaks

木のもとに汁も膾も桜かな

ki no moto ni
shiru mo namasu mo
sakura kana

Beneath the tree
In the soups and the salads
Cherry blossoms everywhere!

やがて死ぬけしきは見えず蝉の声

yagate shinu
keshiki wa miezu
semi no koe

Of its approaching death
The cicada speaks
Not a word

稲妻に悟らぬ人の貴さよ

いなずま　さと　　ひと　　たっと

inazuma ni
satoranu hito no
tattosa yo

Those who see lightning
Without thinking of transience
How admirable!

ひごろ憎き烏も雪の朝哉

にく　からす　ゆき　あしたかな

higoro nikuki
karasu mo yuki no
ashita kana

Even loathsome crows
Are transformed by
Morning snow

初秋や畳みながらの蚊屋の夜着

hatsuaki ya
tataminagara no
kaya no yogi

Early autumn—
A folded mosquito net
For my blanket

梅が香にのっと日の出る山路かな

ume ga ka ni
notto hi no deru
yamaji kana

A whiff of plum blossoms
And up pops the sun—
Mountain path

野ざらしを心に風のしむ身かな

nozarashi o
kokoro ni kaze no
shimu mi kana

Seeing my bones
Laid bare by the wayside
How the wind stings!

ひやひやと壁をふまえて昼寝哉

hiyahiya to
kabe o fumaete
hirune kana

A cool wall
Against my feet
Naptime!

kono michi ya
yuku hito nashi ni
aki no kure

This road—
Travelled by no man
At autumn's twilight

この道やゆく人なしに秋の暮れ

みち　ひと　あき　く

旅に病んで夢は枯野をかけ廻る

tabi ni yande
yume wa kareno o
kakemeguru

Taken ill while travelling
My dreams race over
Withered fields

夏河を越すうれしさよ手に草履

なつかわ こ て ぞうり

natsukawa o
kosu ureshisa yo
te ni zōri

Such joy in crossing
A summer stream
Sandals in hand

春の海終日のたりのたり哉

はる　うみひねもす　　　　　　　かな

haru no umi
hinemosu notari
notari kana

The spring sea
All day rising and
Subsiding

楠の根を静にぬらす時雨哉

くす ね しずか しぐれ かな

kusu no ne o
shizuka ni nurasu
shigure kana

Camphor roots
Noiselessly moistened
By a fine winter rain

古井戸や蚊に飛ぶ魚の音くらし

furuido ya
ka ni tobu sakana no
oto kurashi

An old well—
The murky sound of
A fish leaping for a gnat

harusame ya
koiso no kogai
nururu hodo

A spring shower—
Barely wetting the little shells
On this rocky little shore

春雨や小磯の小貝ぬるゝほど

は
る
さ
め

こ
い
そ

こ
が
い

fuji hitotsu
uzumi nokoshite
wakaba kana

Fuji alone
Floats above
A sea of new leaves

不二ひとつうづみ残して若葉かな

kaya no uchi ni
hotaru hanashite
ā raku ya

Under the mosquito net
Setting fireflies free
Ah, such fun!

蚊帳の内にほたる放してアゝ楽や

みじか夜や毛むしの上に露の玉

mijikayo ya
kemushi no ue ni
tsuyu no tama

A short summer night—
The hairy caterpillar wears
Pearls of dew

一わたしおくれた人にしぐれかな

hitowatashi
okureta hito ni
shigure kana

Late for the ferry
He stands alone in
Drizzling rain

古井戸のくらきに落ちる花椿

ふるいど

お

はなつばき

furuido no
kuraki ni ochiru
hanatsubaki

Falling into the gloom
Of an old well—
A camellia

古池に草履沈みてみぞれ哉

furuike ni
zōri shizumite
mizore kana

In the old pond
A sunken sandal—
Falling sleet

釣鐘にとまりてねむる胡蝶かな

tsurigane ni
tomarite nemuru
kochō kana

Settled on
The temple bell—
A sleeping butterfly

斧入れて香におどろくや冬木立

ono irete
ka ni odoroku ya
fuyu kodachi

A swing of the axe
The scent a revelation
Winter woods

寂として客の絶間のぼたん哉

せき　きゃく　たえま　かな

seki to shite
kyaku no taema no
botan kana

In the quiet lull
Between guests—
Peonies

五月雨や大河を前に家二軒

samidare ya
taiga o mae ni
ie niken

Spring rains—
Two houses stand before
The swollen river

身にしむや亡妻の櫛を閨に踏む

mi ni shimu ya
naki tsuma no kushi o
neya ni fumu

The keen chill
Of my late wife's comb
Underfoot in the bedroom

菜の花や鯨もよらず海暮れぬ

nanohana ya
kujira mo yorazu
umi kurenu

Mustard blossoms—
No whales in the offing
A darkening sea

顔白き子のうれしさよ枕蚊帳

かおしろ

こ

まくらがや

kao shiroki
ko no ureshisa yo
makuragaya

Such joy in watching
My fair-faced child through
The small mosquito net

yamatoji no
miya mo waraya mo
tsubame kana

All along these ancient roads
In shrines and straw houses
Swallows everywhere!

大和路の宮もわら屋もつばめ哉

待人の足音遠き落葉哉

まちびと　あしおと　とお　おちば　かな

machibito no
ashioto tōki
ochiba kana

The one I yearn to meet
A footfall in the distance—
Fallen leaves

桜散る苗代水や星月夜

さくらち　なわしろみず　ほしづきよ

sakura chiru
nawashiro mizu ya
hoshizukiyo

Falling blossoms
Water flowing into seedling beds
A starry night

春雨やものがたりゆく簑と傘

はるさめ

みの　かさ

harusame ya
monogatariyuku
mino to kasa

Gentle spring rain—
Walking lost in conversation
Straw cloak and umbrella

白梅に明くる夜ばかりとなりにけり

shiraume ni
akuru yo bakari to
narinikeri

All that remains
Is the break of dawn
In white plum blossoms

里の子の袂からちる桜かな

sato no ko no
tamoto kara chiru
sakura kana

Spilling from the sleeves
Of the village child—
Cherry petals

うら壁やしがみ付たる貧乏雪
かべ　　　　　　　　　　つい　　　びんぼうゆき

urakabe ya
shigamitsuitaru
binbōyuki

Clinging
To the rear wall
Even the snow is desperate

おとろへや榾折りかねる膝頭

ほ た お

ひ ざ が し ら

otoroe ya
hota orikaneru
hizagashira

Diminished with age—
Unable to break kindling
Over my knee

三文が霞見にけり遠眼鏡

さんもん　かすみみ　　　　　とおめがね

san mon ga
kasumi minikeri
tōmegane

Three coins
For a glimpse of mist
Through the telescope

山寺や雪の底なる鐘の声

やまでら ゆき そこ かね こえ

yamadera ya
yuki no soko naru
kane no koe

Mountain temple—
Beneath the snow
The call of the bell

外は雪内は煤ふる栖かな

そと　ゆき　うち　すす　　すみか

soto wa yuki
uchi wa susu furu
sumika kana

Snowfall outside
Sootfall inside—
Such is home

只一つ耳際に蚊の羽かぜ哉

ただひと みみぎわ か は かな

tada hitotsu
mimigiwa ni ka no
hakaze kana

No breeze but from
The wings of the mosquito
At my ear

門々の下駄の泥より春立ちぬ

かどかど　げた　どろ　はる　た

kadokado no
geta no doro yori
haru tachinu

Spring arrives
In muddy clogs
At every door

冬の蝿逃せば猫にとられけり

fuyu no hae
nigaseba neko
ni torarekeri

The winter fly I spared
Was captured by
The cat

ISSA (1763–1828)

是がまあつひの栖か雪五尺

kore ga mā
tui no sumika ka
yuki goshaku

Is this, then,
Where I live out my days?
Five feet of snow

ゆうぜんとして山を見る蛙かな

yūzen to
shite yama o miru
kawazu kana

So composed
The frog as it regards
The mountain

大の字に寝て涼しさよ寂しさよ

dainoji ni
nete suzushisa yo
sabishisa yo

Sleeping spread-eagled
So refreshing
So lonely

雪とけて村いっぱいの子どもかな

yuki tokete
mura ippai no
kodomo kana

Melting snows
Flood the village
With children

やせ蛙^{がえる}まけるな一茶^{いっさ}これにあり

yasegaeru
makeru na issa
kore ni ari

Scrawny frog
Don't give in
Issa is with you

65

yasegaeru
makeru na issa
kore ni ari

Scrawny frog
Don't give in
Issa is with you

やせ蛙（がえる）まけるな一茶（いっさ）これにあり

蚂の声に馴れてすやすや寝る子哉

ka no koe ni
narete suyasuya
neru ko kana

The hum of mosquitoes
A soothing lullaby to the
Sleeping child

我と来て遊べや親のない雀

われ き あそ おや すずめ

ware to kite
asobe ya oya no
nai suzume

Come
Play with me
Orphaned sparrow

花ふぶき泥わらんじで通りけり

はな　どろ　とお

hana fubuki
doro waranji de
tōrikeri

Passing through
A flurry of petals in
Muddy straw sandals

隅の蜘蛛案じな煤はとらぬぞよ

すみ　くも　あん　　　　すす

sumi no kumo
anji na susu o
toranu zo yo

Spiders in the corners
Fear not, I won't
Be dusting

栗拾ひねんねんころり云ながら

kuri hiroi
nen nen korori
iinagara

Gathering chestnuts
While whispering
Lullabies

小言いふ相手は壁ぞ秋の暮

kogoto iu
aite wa kabe zo
aki no kure

No one to scold
But the wall on an
Autumn evening

ISSA (1763–1828)

古郷は雲の先也秋の暮

ふるさと　くも　さき　なり　あき　　くれ

furusato wa
kumo no saki nari
aki no kure

My home village
Lies just beyond the clouds
Autumn evening

72

花の陰寝まじ未来がおそろしき

はな　かげ　ね　　　　みらい

hana no kage
nemaji mirai ga
osoroshiki

No sleep for me
In blossoms' shade
For fear of what may come

木をつみて夜の明やすき小窓かな

ki o tsumite
yo no ake yasuki
komado kana

A pruned branch
And dawn comes easily
To my little window

74

行く秋にしがみついたる木の葉哉

yuku aki ni
shigamitsuitaru
konoha kana

So desperately
The leaves cling
To the departing fall

紫陽花や壁のくづれをしぶく雨

ajisai ya
kabe no kuzure o
shibuku ame

Hydrangeas—
A crumbling wall
Lashed by rain

月涼し蛙の聲のわきあがる

つきすず かわず こえ

tsuki suzushi
kawazu no koe no
wakiagaru

Cooling moon
A cacophony of
Croaking frogs

生きて帰れ露の命と言ひながら

ikite kaere
tsuyu no inochi to
iinagara

Come back alive
Even if you must talk
Of life's transience

吹きたまる落葉や町の行き止り

fukitamaru
ochiba ya machi no
yukidomari

Swept up by the wind
Heaps of fallen leaves on
Dead end streets

汽車過ぎて烟うづまく若葉かな

kisha sugite
kemuri uzumaku
wakaba kana

The train passes
In a whirl of smoke—
Young leaves

蜘蛛殺すあとの淋しき夜寒哉

kumo korosu
ato no sabishiki
yosamu kana

After killing a spider
Such a cold and
Lonely night

81

銭湯で上野の花の噂かな

sentō de
ueno no hana no
uwasa kana

At the public bath
Gossiping about the
Cherry blossoms of Ueno

次の間の灯も消えて夜寒哉

つぎ　ま　ともし　　き　　　よさむかな

tsugi no ma no
tomoshi mo kiete
yosamu kana

In the next room, too,
The light goes out
Cold night

冬ごもり顔も洗はず書に対す

fuyugomori
kao mo arawazu
sho ni taisu

House-bound in winter
Turning to my books before
Even washing my face

夏虫の死で落ちけり本の上

natsumushi no
shinde ochikeri
hon no ue

A summer insect
Falls dead
Into my book

釣鐘にとまりて光る蛍かな

tsurigane ni
tomarite hikaru
hotaru kana

Settled on
The temple bell—
A glowing firefly

古庭や月に湯婆の湯をこぼす

furuniwa ya
tsuki ni tanpo no
yu o kobosu

The old garden—
A hot water bottle emptied
In the moonlight

汽車道に低く雁飛ぶ月夜哉

きしゃみち
ひく
かり
と
つきよ
かな

kishamichi ni
hikuku kari tobu
tsukiyo kana

Over the rails
Wild geese fly low
On a moonlit night

刃物置いて盗人防ぐ夜寒かな

はものお　ぬすっとふせ　よさむ

hamono oite
nusutto fusegu
yosamu kana

Knife by the bed
Wary of thieves—
A chilly night

蝉の声しばらく汽車に押されけり

せみ こえ きしゃ お

semi no koe
shibaraku kisha ni
osarekeri

Song of the cicada
For a time overwhelmed
By the train

新年の棺に逢ひぬ夜中頃

しんねん ひつぎ あ よなかごろ

shinnen no
hitsugi ni ainu
yonaka goro

A coffin on the
New Year, met
About midnight

島々に灯をともしけり春の海

shimajima ni
hi o tomoshikeri
haru no umi

On every island
Lights have been lit
Spring sea

半日の嵐に折るる葵かな

はんにち　あらし　お　　あおい

hannichi no
arashi ni oruru
aoi kana

Snapped in a
Half-day storm—
Hollyhocks

風呂敷<ruby>ふろしき</ruby>をほどけば柿<ruby>かき</ruby>のころげけり

furoshiki o
hodokeba kaki no
korogekeri

I untied the wrapping cloth
And out tumbled
Persimmons

雪の絵を春も掛けたる埃哉

yuki no e o
haru mo kaketaru
hokori kana

A painting of snow
Still hung come spring
Look at the dust!

牡丹画いて絵の具は皿に残りけり

botan egaite
enogu wa sara ni
nokorikeri

Having painted a peony
The colour remains
In the dish